ANTLIA PNEUMATICA

A play about place, space, grace

Anne Washburn

THEATRE COMMUNICATIONS GROUP   NEW YORK   2019

The publication of *Antlia Pneumatica* by Anne Washburn, through TCG's Book Program, is made possible in part by the New York State Council on the Arts with the support of Governor Andrew Cuomo and the New York State Legislature.

TCG books are exclusively distributed to the book trade by Consortium Book Sales and Distribution.

Library of Congress Control Numbers:
2018057430 (print) / 2019003974 (ebook)
ISBN 978-1-55936-580-2 (trade paper) / ISBN 978-1-55936-895-7 (ebook)
A catalog record for this book is available from the Library of Congress

Cover design and art by Douglas Miller

First Edition, September 2019

ANTLIA PNEUMATICA

BOOKS BY ANNE WASHBURN
PUBLISHED BY TCG

Antlia Pneumatica

Mr. Burns and Other Plays
Also Includes:
I Have Loved Strangers
The Small
10 Out of 12

Vast thanks to the Watts Family, and Eagle's Nest

And to Erik Ehn and his weird silent retreat technology

Dedicated to Exquisite Director Genius Ken Rus Schmoll

ANTLIA
PNEUMATICA

PRODUCTION HISTORY

Antlia Pneumatica premiered at Playwrights Horizons (Tim Sanford, Artistic Director; Leslie Marcus, Managing Director; Carol Fishman, General Manager) in New York City on March 11, 2016. It was directed by Ken Rus Schmoll. The set design was by Rachel Hauck, the costume design was by Jessica Pabst, the lighting design was by Tyler Micoleau, songs were by Anne Washburn and Daniel Kluger, the sound design was by Leah Gelpe, and the production stage manager was Megan Schwarz Dickert. The cast was:

NINA	Annie Parisse
LIZ	April Matthis
ULA	Maria Striar
LEN	Nat DeWolf
ADRIAN	Rob Campbell
BAMA	Crystal Finn
CASEY (recorded voice)	Skylar Dunn
WALLY (recorded voice)	Azhy Robertson

CHARACTERS

NINA
LIZ
ULA (pronounced: You-la)
LEN
ADRIAN
BAMA

All are in their late thirties/early forties.

CASEY and WALLY, seven and five, are only heard, never seen. And the scenes in which the adults interact with them are also only heard.

THE PLACE

A ranch in Texas Hill Country.

THE SET

A granite kitchen island. Faced front. Stools.

Floor of polished concrete.

Upstage: the trunk and lower branches of a massive pecan tree.

NOTE

Words in brackets are thought but not spoken.

Someone is digging into a metal bowl of ice cubes in the freezer.

A pitcher of lemonade with ice cubes is stirred vigorously.

Ice cubes jingle gently as a full glass of lemonade is carried across the lodge.

The phone rings.

The jingling trajectory shifts.

The phone rings.

NINA: Yello.

    Mini beat.

    Adrian.

Really?

Mini beat.

How did you know I was here?

*Nina has appeared onstage, a cordless phone in one hand,
the glass of lemonade in the other.*

Don who?

No.

Oh. Yes. Don. Don. Right. How did *Don* . . . find out?

No not Suzie. Definitely not. *(A sudden thought)* Don isn't
coming is he?

Uh-huh. Yeah that's probably better. *(Irrelevantly)* How *is*
Don?

She hears herself, makes a face.

Oh, that's great.

Beat.

Of course. No of course. You're welcome to. Of course. Do
you remember the way?

When do you uh

Okay, great. Yes. *(Again: not relevant)* We can feed you;
we're making a lot of food.

Hears herself, makes face.

All right, *(Waves)* bye.

She stands there for a moment. Utterly blank.

Then turns. Looks offstage. Gears herself up to say something:

As she walks offstage

Near panic:

Liz!

Sound of a plunge

Sound of someone surfacing, gasping

LIZ: Cold! Cold cold cold! Good! Cold!

Sound of splashing.

Nina speaks alone to the audience:

NINA: I was standing in my cabin and the Sphinx . . . thing, was at the back door.

The curtain was blowing in front of it, I couldn't see it clearly but there was

and I don't know where the light was coming from, but

mane, flank, but then a moment of profile, not maw but sharp: nose, lips, jaw—a woman.

And I turned and I was surprised to find that the front door, the door to the meadow with the quote unquote pecan orchard was wide open and the light was just breaking

And I thought it was the wind had blown it open because in the dream there was this incredible wind the night before.

I stepped forward to close the front door, or to walk through it, and I woke up and it was the middle of the night it had cooled off. I pulled the blanket up from the foot of the bed and went back to sleep.

A bird cheep, very loud, like a small cheep heard right up close, like a little bird leaning into your ear and letting loose.

Another cheep.

A saucy trill.

Lights change.

The island is spread with cookbooks, notes, a few bowls and ingredients already in play.

Ula and Liz are looking out through the window toward the river, talking about a mostly red bird and what it is.

ULA: Sometimes birds like that are loud.
LIZ: I think birds which have just the tiniest piece of red on them are the loudest I've noticed that. They're louder than all-red birds.
ULA: I guess they have something to prove.

Sees Nina, waves list.

Really? We're really making all this food?

NINA: It's a funeral Ula. Funeral spells food.

ULA: Yeah but who is this for? Just the eight of us.

LIZ: Nine.

ULA: I love to eat, don't get me wrong.

NINA: I thought you liked cooking.

ULA: I do. I do. I'm thrilled.

NINA: We're going to make a feast.

ULA: We are indeed.

NINA: But get a swim in first. Liz jumped off the edge of the Blue Hole.

ULA: Finally.

LIZ *(Doesn't love this)*: It's very high up, and it's very frightening. And, it is not a natural thing to do, to jump into water which you cannot see the bottom of.

NINA: So Major. Your whole life.

LIZ: You were not an early adopter of the Blue Hole leap either, might I add.

NINA: Our whole childhood was our mom telling us absolutely not to jump into the Blue Hole from the edge—

LIZ: Which *she* always did

NINA: Which she always did! And she spent all the years after that telling us to for god's sake jump, just jump, what were we so chicken about.

ULA: It *is* sort of exciting.

NINA: You had the benefit of first coming to it as an adult-sized person, and on mushrooms.

LIZ: Oh god oh god oh god don't tell me, I don't want to think, you jumped into the Blue Hole tripping and was it even daytime?

ULA: There wasn't even a moon.

NINA: We had flashlights.

ULA: Yeah but they weren't trained at the water at the time; I sort of guessed.

NINA: Oh did you do that?

LIZ: Okay there's a rocky ledgy thing . . .

NINA: Yeah I'm glad I didn't know that at the time.

LIZ: And then, but okay but that's fine, that's fine it already happened. Don't tell me anymore. You're alive, that's what counts. You're alive. I'm alive.

NINA *(Going off)*: No one has ever drowned at the Blue Hole.

LIZ: It probably hasn't been given a real chance.

Refrigerator door opening.

NINA *(From off)*: Where did all the eggs go??

LIZ: You made that big scramble this morning.

NINA: I didn't use all of the eggs. There was that big pink carton.

ULA: Oh those eggs were very ancient. I tossed them.

NINA: Oh really?

ULA: They were months old, they were from March.

NINA *(Coming back into the room)*: Oh, I didn't realize that. Liz I thought you brought them.

LIZ: Uh uh.

NINA: That must be when our cousin was out here. I guess no one's been out here since then.

ULA: So this place just sits here.

NINA: I know, it is sort of a pity. Well everyone's in L.A. or New York, and it's a pain to get to.

What do we need eggs for, just about every bakey thing there is.

LIZ: Plus big scrambles in the morning.

NINA: We have bacon right?

LIZ: Lots and lots of bacon.

ULA: You also have twenty jars of mustard.

NINA: Twenty? No.

ULA: You've got seven in the door. There are probably more in the back. You have doubles of a few brands.

NINA: It's such a pain to drive back and forth. People just shop when they're heading in from the airport. Really what we need is a fridge cam.

ULA: What you need is internet.

LIZ: Right?!

NINA: Yeah . . .

ULA: Should I start by cleaning the fridge of every suspect item? We need the space anyway.

NINA: Mustard doesn't go bad.

ULA: Eggs go bad. All kinds of things go bad. I never know about mayo. You've got like six jars of mayo. I may just cull some of them, to feel like the situation is under control.

NINA: I would have asked you to bring eggs, this is such a bummer.

ULA: Call Len.

NINA: Len's past Kerrville by now, for sure. We'll do another big shop but I thought we could do the baking tonight so the kitchen wouldn't be so hot tomorrow.

LIZ *(Pointedly)*: What about Adrian.

ULA: Adrian.

NINA: I don't have his number.

I didn't ask.

ULA: Adrian?

LIZ: Adrian's coming.

NINA: Yeah I needed to have mentioned that earlier.

ULA: When is he . . . where is he . . .

Arms twirling around in the air in slow-mo to indicate more questions than are possible given the limitations of time and space and language

finally settles on:

I didn't realize you were in touch.

NINA: We're not. He called me up. On the road. And said he'd
be here in a few hours.

ULA: He just called you right up.

NINA: Uh-huh.

ULA: And you said . . . yes? . . . come on by?

NINA: I was flustered.

ULA *(To Liz)*: Adrian's coming.

LIZ: I *know*.

NINA: It's been sixteen years. Who cares.

ULA: Time is an illusion, my friend.

LIZ: She's right. Time *is* an illusion.

NINA: Oh fuck you.

ULA: You haven't one bit talked with him in sixteen years.

NINA: Well I a bit of; no.

ULA: You

NINA: No. I haven't

ULA: You what.

LIZ: When was it?

NINA: No. Basically no. I got drunk one night, two years after.

LIZ *(Helpfully)*: Fourteen years ago.

NINA: And I called him. *(To Liz, stricken)* How did I have his
number? *Amelia*.

LIZ: Amelia gave it to you. 'Cause she's an enabler.

ULA *(Remembering Amelia)*: *Amelia*, right. Amelia.

NINA: And we had a really bad conversation. And *that* was the
last time I spoke with him. But that was, yes, fourteen years
ago.

ULA: Those never go well. You didn't please tell me you
didn't . . .

NINA: In my head it was: you know, I've healed, I've moved on,
I'm dating this very nice man

ULA: Was that Adam?

NINA: That was Trent.

LIZ *(Still helpful)*: Right before Adam.

ULA: Why don't I remember Trent?

LIZ: Trent was like:

She snaps her fingers.

ULA: Oh right. Trent. Of course. Trent.

NINA: Trent was great.

ULA: Yeees. So you were like I'm dating this Trent person, I don't care—

NINA: —can't we talk about this like adults. I believe I used the word closure.

ULA: Yeah I know that phone call. Uh. So awful.

NINA: Yeah, he wasn't having it. He was like: this is bullshit. I was like: *you're* bullshit.

ULA: Which is accurate.

NINA: Which, yes. Yes. So that was that phone call.

ULA: And now he's here.

NINA: Yup. In a few hours.

ULA: Excellent. Really great.

NINA: He's here for the funeral.

ULA: Oh.

NINA: They were so close.

ULA: Were they back in touch??

NINA: He heard about it from Don.

ULA: Don?

NINA: You remember, Don was Adrian's kind of strange creepy housemate for a while, back in Austin.

LIZ: Oh Don Don Don with the *hair*, right?

NINA: Right.

ULA: He didn't hear about it from Don. Don's dead.

NINA: Don?

ULA: Don's dead he died . . . *(Ticking it back)* you guys had left town already. Fourteen years ago? Fifteen years ago?

NINA: Don *died?*

ULA: He got tangled up with . . . it wasn't a drug deal but it was with drug deal type of people—was it, did it have something to do with ticket scalping? I can't remember. I just remember it was shady, and kind of strange, and he went off in a car with someone and that was the last anyone saw of him.

NINA: How come I don't know this?

ULA: I think this was when you and I weren't speaking.

Liz has been tracking something internally.

LIZ *(This is only a very mild crisis)*: Oh you guys, this is awful: I don't care.

NINA *(Only mildly engaged by this)*: You might be kind of in shock or something.

LIZ: Maybe. I think I just don't care.

ULA: I know. His parents were super sad. That was the strange thing. Barely knowing Don and not liking him at all and then seeing his super sad parents.

NINA: Adrian said Don was selling real estate in Corpus Christi. And all over the Gulf. He said he was doing really well.

ULA: Maybe he didn't mean the same Don.

NINA: Maybe . . . there isn't another Don. Did they find the body? Or did he just go off in a car?

ULA: Oh, um . . . yeah. They did find the body. They did it was. I don't remember how. It was some kind of a bad way and, I think I might be getting it mixed up with a movie, how they found his body.

NINA: And it was definitely his body.

ULA: Oh, yeah, I mean, he still had a face.

NINA: That's so . . . strange. I mean, isn't it?

Car horn. Tires on gravel. They all jump a little.

ULA: Think that's him?

Little beat.

NINA: I think that's Len. Adrian was never a honker.
ULA: Sixteen years. A person can *become* a honker.

Len enters.

LEN *(This is general, the last bit directed at Nina)*: You know
    what I found, in my glove compartment on the drive here,
    one of your dad's Best-Of's.
ULA: Which one?
LEN: Volume Two: "Oldies. Goodies." Where he has that beard
    on the cover.
ULA: Oh I like that one.
LEN: And that guitar, that guitar which used to be around here
    is it still here?
NINA: No. Len when was the last time you cleaned out your
    glove compartment?
LEN: No no, I listen to it sometimes, it's part of my collection.
    I've been blasting it.
ULA: Is that an actual cassette? Give that here. It's been a long
    time since I handled a cassette you still play these?
LEN: I didn't want to buy all new CDs when I already owned the
    cassette why should I.
ULA: Sound quality.
LEN: I don't care about sound quality I'm not one of those peo-
    ple, I just listen to the song. Should I put it on?
NINA: No.

On the overhead speaker:

*Two small children—a girl, seven, and a boy, five—sing
simultaneously, and with increasing volume;*

Occasionally, they try to drown each other out:

CASEY:	WALLY:
Michael row, your boat	
	Row row row
Ashore	
	Your boat
Hallelujah	
	Gently down
Michael row	
	The stream
Your boat ashore	
	Merrily
Hallelujah	
	Merrily
The River Jordan	
	Merrily merrily
IS WIDE AND DEEP	
	ROW ROW
HALLELUJAH	
	ROW!
Many miles	
	ROW ROW
Before I sleep	
	ROW!
HALLELUJAH	
	Merrily
Michael row	
	Merrily
Row row your boat!	
	Merrily
HALLELUJAH	
	MERRILY
Michael row your boat!	
	MERRILY
Row row	
	MERRILY

CASEY: WALLY:
Your boat ashore!

                                        ROW

HALLELUJAH

                                          ROW

RIVER JORDAN!

                                          ROW

It overflow!

                                          ROW

Sinner row

                                          ROW

To save your soul!

                                          ROW!

MICHAEL ROW

                                          ROW!

YOUR BOAT

                                          YOUR BOAT

ASHORE

                                          GENTLY

HALLELUJAH

                                          HALLELUJAH

MICHAEL ROW

                                          MERRILY

YOUR BOAT

                                          MERRILY

ASHORE

                                          MERRILY

HALLELUJAH

                                          HALLELUJAH

HALLELUJAH   HALLELUJAH

                                          LIFE IS BUT A DREAM!

Night. Crickets and frogs outside.

Screen door opens, bangs slightly shut.

ULA: Adrian!

ADRIAN: Hello . . . everybody.

ULA: I didn't hear your car. Did anyone hear the car?

ADRIAN: I walked.

NINA: Not from San Antonio.

ADRIAN: No. I was starved. Stopped off at Rudy's for some
   BBQ. Actually ran into a guy I know from Albuquerque
   I had some business with. I called, but nobody answered.

NINA: We were swimming, probably.

ULA: Still no answering machine.

NINA: Dad was adamant and, I don't know.

LIZ: Dad wouldn't have cared. That was his own thing and he
   knew it.

NINA *(Nerves, although you can't really tell. Talking)*: Let's
   hang on to every tradition. We don't have enough here; we
   are not rooted to this glorious land. Let's make whims into
   traditions, bad habits into traditions. Where are you walking from?

ADRIAN: From the turnoff. From that gravel section, where
   I always thought I'd spin out.

NINA: You spun out?

ADRIAN: No I just broke down. No reason. I tried to call again
   but no cell service.

LEN: Still the middle of nowhere. Good to know, right. Where
   that is. It's right. Here.

ULA: So you've been walking for

ADRIAN: About an hour.

NINA: The guys at the garage aren't there until the morning.

ADRIAN: I'll call them in the morning.

There's a little pause which he seems comfortable with.

LEN: Wine?

ADRIAN: Yes, thanks.

ULA: There's guac and fried chicken and coleslaw left.

ADRIAN: I'm good.

LEN: It's actually sangria.

ADRIAN: Sounds fine.

LEN: Which I now suddenly remember you hate.

ADRIAN: I like the taste. I used to think it was emasculating.

LEN: No more.

ADRIAN: Now I think lots of other things are emasculating. Sangria is just wine with fruit in it.

NINA: Oh and we're out of ice cubes.

LEN: So it's lukewarm sangria.

ADRIAN: I was parched.

LEN: I'll get you another glass.

There's another little pause.

ULA: So where are you living these days, are you down by the
Gulf?

ADRIAN: No, I'm actually in Arizona.

LEN: Oh, Phoenix?

ADRIAN: No. His mom coming to this?

NINA: She died a few years ago.

ADRIAN: Oh I'm sorry to hear that. I always liked Mariela. What
about his sisters?

NINA: Allison died ten years ago from some kind of very strange
blood disorder. Jenny's in Alaska and wasn't interested in
coming. It's just us.

ADRIAN: Us.

This all that's left?

NINA: Suzie is coming. Scott and Peg and Bama.

ADRIAN: Bama. Scott. Peg. Amazing.

Don said you have the body.

NINA: The ashes. Peg is picking them up today in New York—
that's where he was living—

ULA: So *Don* told you about Sean.

ADRIAN: Yeah. I thought he heard from Suzie but Nina says no.

NINA: It wasn't a romance it was more, just, Don hovering around.

ADRIAN: That's too bad. I know he thought about her a lot.

ULA: Nina says Don is doing well. Real estate.

ADRIAN: Adulthood suits him. And success, I guess. He's
slimmed down. He's a little hard.

But he's a lot easier to talk with. Much better conversationalist.

ULA: I have real-estate questions, do you think he'd mind if
I contacted him or is he too big for the old crowd?

ADRIAN: I don't think he'd bend over backward, but I bet you
could get a tip or two off of him.

ULA: That would be great, will you pass me his number?

ADRIAN: It's on his site. Shore Estates.

ULA: Oh great. Thanks.

ADRIAN: Should I write it down, or?

ULA: I can remember. Thanks.

ADRIAN: So you all stayed in touch. With Sean.

There's a kind of a pause.

LIZ: No. Not really.

NINA: We'd definitely. From time to time. When he came to
town.

LEN: For a while. Every now and then. A drunken phone call.
Really *fun* drunken phone calls, we'd talk for hours. Then
less fun drunken phone calls. Then he went into AA. Then
we spoke less often.

ULA: He didn't have a will but he had a file. Called: When I Die.
Which they found in his things. And in it he said he wanted

to be buried here. The file was years and years and years old but no one else . . . claimed him, so.

NINA: He was seeing someone but it was very new, his ex wasn't on great terms with him and they didn't have any kids; he did have a lot of friends and they're having a big memorial for him in New York but they didn't expect the body so there wasn't a . . . jurisdictional dispute.

LEN: It didn't say anything about a tombstone did it? The file?

NINA: Gravestone.

LEN: If he's buried here? Isn't it a tombstone?

NINA: I think you have to earn a tombstone. I don't think a few years kicking around Austin counts.

Should he have one?

LEN: Shouldn't he?

NINA: Well not if you're scattered, right? You're sort of everywhere. You can't be pinned down. To one location or sentiment.

LEN *(Just occurring to him)*: Did he say where? He didn't say where did he. The Blue Hole?

NINA: He didn't say. I was thinking maybe near the Blue Hole, like just before sunset when there's that last bit of light, like kind of up a bit on the hill or

LEN: In the shrubbery

LIZ: Scrub.

LEN: Scrub. Right. Is that dignified enough? To be scattered in scrub?

ULA: There's still no way up on that mesa, is there.

NINA: Butte. No. They're stubborn, about that butte.

LIZ: They have the butte, we have the Blue Hole, it's a kind of standoff of Western land desirables

LEN: But you win, right?

LIZ: Oh totally. I mean, a butte is great, a vista is amazing but, it's *hot*.

NINA: Dad was always trying to befriend the guy whose family owns the butte, so he could eventually challenge him to a winner-take-all drinking contest. He was like: I've got twenty years on that guy, he'll never suspect a thing.

LIZ: He never came close.

NINA: He never came close. He's a Seventh-Day Adventist, right? Or a Jehovah's. One of those nondrinking ones he didn't even want to talk with Dad, he was all: I *know who you are*, sir.

LIZ: Which thrilled Dad.

NINA: He was thrilled. "Sixty-five years of age and somebody still thinks I'm a Bad Boy."

ULA: It's just too bad you couldn't work out some kind of pass-through situation right?

NINA: Yeah but no one wants anyone else hanging out on their butte or in their Blue Hole.

LIZ: That was so almost obscene.

LEN: Yeah if it were called:

NINA: No no!

Or, wait, god, I'm sorry—slipped into mom mode for a sec. Go right ahead.

ADRIAN: Kids?

NINA: Two. Boy/girl. Five/seven. But they're fast asleep in their cabin. If it were called?

LEN: It wasn't good enough to sustain the delay. Obscenity is a dish best served piping hot.

NINA: Oh Len

ULA: Len!

NINA: I'm sorry. Really?

LEN: Really.

NINA: Now we'll never know

LEN: Gonna take it to my grave. *Unless, I* ask to be scattered here as well and have it as my epitaph.

NINA: You're welcome to do both.

ULA: Just make sure it's in your When I Die file.

LEN: If I had an If I Die file that would be the first thing. The epitaph. I should make up an epitaph. I should make up an If I Die File shouldn't I.

ULA: You should. You're gonna die.

LEN: Right. I *am* going to die, aren't I.

NINA: And when it happens. You don't want someone else coming up with your epitaph.

LIZ: And it could happen at any moment. It could happen in the next second.

LEN: That's *right.*

LIZ: Everyone just, just: be quiet for, for just a second.

They're all quiet, the second passes.

And we're fine. But it could have happened that quickly, right then.

NINA: I mean . . . yes . . .

LIZ: Tornado, rattler in the cupboard, aneurism. Heart attack— *(Directly to the audience)* And for you ladies you need to know it's more common among women than you'd think. *(She returns her attention to the room)* Ah—

LEN: Wolf.

LIZ: Wolf. Gunshot—someone could be standing right outside there, we'd never see them in the dark. Ah—

LEN: Nuclear conflagration.

LIZ: Yes.

NINA *(Interrupting this)*: But Len you do have a will, right?

LEN: I do have a will I mean, yes. I have a financial document. But I don't have anything in the way of further instructions. I am going . . . to die. Huh.

And you . . . are going to die. And you. Adrian, do you have a will? Do you have a file?

Minor hitch.

NINA *(Suddenly remembering)*: You have a tattoo. On your stomach. It says:

Remembering:

When I die: torch me where I fall. Let the wind take me.

Adrian laughs.

LEN: Serious?
ULA: Show me.

He laughs.

NINA: It's not a real tattoo it's a
ADRIAN: It was a sort of topic, between us.
NINA: It was a projected tattoo.
ADRIAN: I wanted it to be large. And I couldn't decide on the script. So I waffled.
NINA: It was going to be painful. It was going to be very very painful, the abdomen the entire abdomen. Big thick letters.
ADRIAN: Which at the time, made it seem like an even better idea. But I was broke.
NINA: There was that one night.
ADRIAN: Oh.
NINA: You were really drunk.
ADRIAN: I was really drunk.
NINA: You were going to sell your motorcycle, to that guy at La Zona Rosa, at the corner table, and then march over to the tattoo shop.
ADRIAN: She knocked me unconscious with a whiskey bottle to prevent this.
NINA: I didn't do that but I did do something, what was it.
ADRIAN: I don't remember any of this.

NINA: Oh! Right. I got you more to drink. I got you more to drink. I said: great idea. Let's celebrate it. I got you two more shots and you passed out. It was brilliant. Usually I tried to reason with you. That never worked.

ADRIAN: No.

Little pause.

ULA: Your dad is here, right? Does he have an epitaph?

NINA: No. Unmarked grave. Unmarked!

LIZ: Really obnoxious.

NINA: Too cool for school.

LIZ: Mom has a gravestone.

NINA: With a Bible verse. Selected by Dad.

LEN: What was it?

LIZ:

> Who is this that cometh out of the
> Wilderness like pillars of smoke
> Perfumed with Myrrh and Frankincense.

LEN: That's lovely.

NINA: It's very lovely. I'm not convinced that it's accurate.

ULA: I don't know that they're about summing you up. I think they're more about getting people in the right mood to contemplate you.

NINA: Regardless. And she would not have liked the Bible part at all.

LIZ: But she didn't leave a file.

NINA: She didn't leave a file. So.

A moment.

People come up with epitaphs.

As they progress, they're a little bit captured by something.

LEN:

> Here lies me
> Now all that you see

NINA:

> Now I'm dead
> Ashes are my head
> Worms are my bones
> My eyes are stones

LEN:

> Alone. I am enriched by the dark.

LIZ:

> Sweet days are all behind me
> And giddy nights
> The icy shifting singing reaches
> Are my delights
> I could die endlessly
> I drink these sights

ULA:

> And now I am translucent
> And the world is gold I left
> The iron on the pot at boil batter half
> mixed the cat unfed the
>
> > > wolf
> > >
> > > > bold
> in the center of the living room
>
> The baby in its jaw

I flickered and I turned to go
And as I exited waved slow
ly at all, goodbye to all, my eyes
the last to vanish, fixed,
on that flecked and foaming maw.

They're released.

LEN: What about the novel. Did they find that? In Sean's stuff?
NINA: No.
ULA: I asked.
LEN: All those short stories?
ULA: Nothing. He must have just chucked them all out. At some
point.
LIZ: Really?
ULA: I don't have any copies. Of any of them. I must have, some
move. Do you?
LEN: No, me neither. Huh.

Well.

I always thought . . .
ULA: I know. Me too.

Bit of a quiet.

LEN: Well.

Got to get my dose of night sky.
ULA: Oh me too. Are there any blankets that aren't mothbally?
LIZ: I did not remember to demothballize the blankets.
NINA: Awww. Liz.
LEN: I don't think I think a night sky is the same without the
scent of mothballs.

ULA: I don't like it at all. But I like it better than jackrabbit poop
  stuck to my back.

  You want to?
NINA: I'm good. I gave them all a good hard stare last night.
ULA: Alright. Don't, uh, finish up all of the wine.

  They troop out.

  Liz lingers for a moment in the doorway.

LIZ: Hey Adrian, what do you think, Time an Illusion?

  We were having a discussion about it, before you arrived.

  A micro-moment.

ADRIAN: No. Time is . . . crushingly heavy. And solid. And real.
LIZ: Huh. Alright.

  She goes.

  Adrian and Nina.

ADRIAN: It was a mistake to come?
NINA: No. Of course not.
ADRIAN: It's been a long time.
NINA: It *has* been a long time.

  There is a bit of a pause.

  You know it's weird I don't think. I don't know that I would
  have recognized you, if we'd passed on the street.
ADRIAN: Haggard.
NINA: No. Just. I don't know.

I see you better the longer you're in my vicinity, like, eyes adjusting to [the light]

ADRIAN: The dark.

NINA: Sure.

ADRIAN *(Immediately)*: Those kids immaculate?

NINA: Huh? Oh, do you mean—

ADRIAN: -ly. Conceived.

NINA *(A little nervous)*: Yeah they're not tidy. Or in any way pristine, well he's still a little pristine, he still has that baby star fluff around him a little, sheer ignorance, it's adorable, she's mayhem, but no, I had them in congress with my husband, Adam.

ADRIAN: And who is Adam?

NINA: Not sure that I can just sum him up.

ADRIAN: Fair enough.

NINA: This is the point where you say he's a lucky man.

ADRIAN: I don't think I know enough about him.

Mini beat.

NINA: Fair enough.

What about you? Kids? Wife?

On his silence.

Ex-wife/*two* ex-wifes?

Three.

ADRIAN: Uh uh.

NINA: You must be seeing somebody.

ADRIAN: I'm not.

NINA: Just . . . catting around?

ADRIAN: Uh uh.

NINA: Uh uh?

ADRIAN: Nope.

NINA: Huh.

ADRIAN: You're having a moment where . . . you wonder if I've been thinking about you. You wonder if I've come to tell you that. And the answer is no.

NINA: Ummm . . .

ADRIAN: I haven't forgotten you. But you're a memory. Not something real.

Not part of my present.

NINA: Okay: yes. Ditto. But.

I actually am. At the moment. Part of your present.

I do not *mean*, *anything* by this, I'm just saying: factually.

ADRIAN: Right.

NINA: Part of your present.

ADRIAN: You and your, keen insistence on facts. Rational process. All coming back.

You know, when I heard about Sean, and this . . . gathering, my thought, my very first thought was, just, habit: Awww. I want my buddy. And my girl.

He laughs.

NINA: And you, a guest in my household.

ADRIAN: Let's join them. You can't really see the sky in L.A. can you.

NINA: No not with the glare.

It's kind of a crazy shame.

ADRIAN: Not at all. Just a city doing its job: protecting you from the obvious.

Let's go.

Outdoors. It is pitch black. A semi-circle, a motley assortment of flashlights and a few candles. Nina is present though she does not speak.

LEN: There was the night we all got so drunk and went outside to look at the stars and wanted to work out the constellations but we couldn't really and kept arguing over which one was Scorpius and Sean was sure it was *(Points)* there and I was positive it was *(Points)* there and there was an epic battle of star-knowledge-posturing but we looked it up in the morning and it turned out neither one of us was right.

BAMA: There was the night the turkey was over-smoked and fell apart I am not shitting you fell apart to the touch which is in theory a good thing but in this case was basically gruesome.

LIZ: The night we were certain we had seen a UFO.

LEN: A *pair* of UFOs, operating in tandem.

ULA: There was that woman in town it was so random we were having a perfectly normal conversation until with no indication at all that the topic was veering she begins discussing the two separate species of aliens kept underground in a vast bunker on government lands in Dulce New Mexico; she and her boyfriend wanted to sneak over there to take a look, but it was supposed to be hard to do, and dangerous, because not only was the government involved but they had allowed certain sections of the bunker to operate autonomously. And if they caught you the species would decide your fate for themselves.

LIZ: That one night I dreamed I was awake, and I was standing in the cabin in the middle of the room, and I looked out at the lawn and the so-called pecan orchard was all grown and enormous and the wind was up and there was this din of just, wind swoosh, and I went to the doorway and I looked up at the sky and there were all these falling stars, and I was really enjoying it for a while until after a while I was like, stop, that is just too many falling stars, I know that there are hundreds of millions and billions and even trillions and probably billions of trillions of stars but I do not know that the sky can sustain that kind of attrition. And sure enough, after a while, there were holes here and there, there were gaps, blank places, and the stars were falling across the sky like rain now, like a heavy blinding rain you can barely even see through and every now and then it would ease up and you'd see the loss, the gappage, I couldn't bear it and I woke up and I lay there and finally I pulled aside the curtains and looked outside but it was an overcast night and so the sky was just like a dark, lead. Doubt lay heavy upon me as I went back to sleep.

LEN: There was the night I woke up, tears streaming down my face, and I didn't know why. And then I thought maybe I did know why. But then I thought better to not know.

Sounds:

Wind in the trees, wild.

The tin roof, rattling slightly.

A curtain, flapping.

Nina gasps awake.

Sees him.

Gasps.

This is just heard on the overhead speaker:

NINA: What are you doing.

ADRIAN: Watching you.

NINA: Watching me . . . sleep?

ADRIAN: Watching over you.

Pause.

NINA: The kids come in. A lot. If they have a nightmare or get scared in their cabin and think they see a spider or

They could come in here.

Did they come in here.

ADRIAN: No one's come in.

NINA: They'd tell Adam. I mean. Obviously. It would be news.

ADRIAN: I'm just over here.

NINA: In my cabin.

ADRIAN: Some story. Just. Make something up.

A bit of a beat.

NINA: The big surprise of parenting, for me, was how much your kids don't believe what you tell them.

ADRIAN: Let me sit next to you. Okay?

NINA: No.

No.

You'd better go.

A small pause.

ADRIAN: Alright.

The next morning. Ula at the island, frozen in a small sea of dough, flour, looking offstage. Nina enters, looking around, is about to say something when Ula holds up a warning hand.

Nina freezes.

Ula beckons her to move forward carefully, which she does.

ULA: Fox.
NINA: Oooh.

They watch it pick its way away.

That's rare. I wish the kids had seen that.
ULA: It looked very businesslike. Wonder what it was up to.
NINA *(Weirdly urgent)*: Hey where is Casey? I thought she was in here.
ULA: She's on the porch with Len.
NINA: You sure?
ULA: Yeah I saw them out there fifteen minutes ago. He's regaling her with tales of the *(Pronouncing the "e")* Olde West.

Nina goes off, to check, comes back. Gets a coffee. Joins Ula.

NINA: Pies, eh?
ULA: As per *Der Plan.*

Ula gestures toward the meadow.

I'm not wrong, right? That pecan orchard is the exact same size it was fifteen years ago.
NINA: You are wrong. It is a *lot* bigger.
ULA: *Is* it?

NINA: Yes, I mean of course it is. Definitely bigger.

ULA: Maybe you got dwarf pecans by mistake.

NINA: No they just, they just need a lot of water, that's why *(Gesturing to the river view)* those wild guys are practically in the river. And that much water is expensive out here. Wilson was the one who was really gung ho about pecans, and the pecan market and he got Dad jacked up about it, and then he did the cost benefit or whatever ratio and then he retired anyway.

ULA: So they're just . . .

NINA: They're in kind of a limbo. I guess. If we were honest about it. Which we try not to be.

Where we're watering them enough to keep them alive

ULA: But not enough to actually become a magnificent pecan orchard.

NINA: Yeah . . . I don't know; they're just kind of in slow-mo. They'll get there, eventually.

ULA: Will they?

NINA: Well we don't want to kill them. They didn't ask to be planted there.

ULA: No.

NINA: It's a kind of a life, right? I mean, they know no other way.

ULA: Unless they're looking over at those guys by the river. And thinking, *that's* living.

NINA: Hopefully, they're not. Hopefully they figure the life they're leading is a perfectly fine one.

ULA: As do we all.

NINA: *Sure.*

How'd you sleep?

ULA: Like gangbusters. I lay there and it was so quiet. And that wind. And do you know I've never slept in those cabins alone?

NINA: Never?

ULA: Not once. Mostly there was Rory. And that one time there
was . . . oh . . .

NINA: . . . um . . .

ULA: *Hammond.*

NINA: *Right.*

ULA: I lay there and I realized I've never been alone in one of
these things. And I thought it's so dark. It's so quiet. That
wind is so spooky. This is actually so awful. And the roof is
rattling. And what if there's big spiders in the beams. And
what if the roof shakes and they lose their balance and they
slip. And then I fell right asleep. And I slept like crazy. And
then I woke up. I think I dreamed a ton though. Probably
about spiders.

NINA: I woke up. In the middle of the night. And Adrian was
sitting in my cabin. On the chair by the window, the rocking chair.

Ula stops working.

ULA: Oh holy god.

NINA: He was holding a lantern and he was looking at me. And
I said,

ULA: A *lantern?*

NINA: Yes, like a. A camping lantern, one of those hurricane
lanterns.

ULA: Never mind. He's in your cabin. Jesus.

NINA: So he's in my cabin and I said, you know, what, what are
you doing here—the kids might come in. And we had a . . .
strange discussion about parenting . . . and he said could he
come sit next to me, on the bed, and I said no, you know,
you'd better go. And so he went. I was kind of terrified.

ULA: Right. No doubt. The fucker.

NINA: And I woke up this morning and I thought shit, you know,
this is sort of major.

ULA *(Restrains herself)*: Uh-huh.

NINA: And I looked over, to where he was sitting, in the rocking chair, and the rocking chair wasn't there. And that was very jarring, because he was rocking back and forth, slightly, the whole time we were talking, the chair was squeaking just that little bit

And I thought he came and took it while I was sleeping? That would be so . . . creepy and weird.

ULA: *Extra* creepy and weird.

NINA: And then I remembered: that rocking chair is gone. It broke. Adam chopped it up last winter and we burned it.

ULA: But—wait.

NINA: So it was a *dream.*

ULA: It was a dream.

NINA: It was just a dream.

ULA: All of it was a dream?

NINA: No the whole thing.

ULA: Okay but—

NINA: I had no idea you would epically freak out.

ULA: Of *course* I was freaking out.

NINA: No I just thought

ULA: Why didn't you say it was a dream?

NINA: I was trying to draw you in to my experience of the event as a little bit of a harmless conversational whatsit. I mean of *course* it was a dream.

ULA: Is it *really* of course? *Really?*

NINA: Yes. Of course it's of course. Jesus.

ULA *(Spots this)*: Then why have a dream . . . in the first place?

NINA: Because we're all . . . here . . . again, and my mind *goes* places. I mean, surely that is natural.

ULA *(Reluctantly has to concede this)*: Uh-huh.

NINA: I'm going to make a pretty lattice crust for this one.

ULA: Are you.

Liz hops in from the outside.

LIZ: Ow. Ow. Ow. Ow. Ow.

NINA: What? What? Where?

ULA: Liz? You okay?

LIZ *(As she's hopping off toward the bathroom)*: Splinters! Splinters!

NINA: Why are you hopping on it?? You're driving them deeper in!!

LIZ: I'm hopping on the good parts of my foot. That are left.

She hops back in with tweezers, sits on a stool, holds her foot up to inspect.

NINA: Here, do you want me to . . .

LIZ: No.

NINA: You sure? Because it's hard—

LIZ: No. Oh no. Back off.

NINA: That was thirty-five years ago.

LIZ: Back away. I remember it, like it was yesterday. Ow.

NINA: Let me—

LIZ: No.

NINA: Literally, it was thirty-five years ago.

LIZ: I was so young, and so tender.

NINA: You know, I was little too! There was just not a lot of precision to be had!

LIZ: Why be a hero? That's my question. Why not just kick back and watch cartoons.

NINA: So Liz comes in one morning, in *agony*, from the yard

LIZ: I don't remember how I got all those splinters

NINA: She has all these splinters

LIZ: No idea

NINA: It wasn't really a yard, it was a little concrete patio

ULA: This isn't Laurel Canyon.

NINA: This was in Encino this little apartment right off a big commercial strip. We moved to Laurel Canyon a year later.

LIZ: I think there must have been a stick or something, blown into the yard. Like, bark.

NINA: But my parents were still asleep and, they could sleep until one P.M. They did that lots of times. So I ran the house in the morning.

LIZ: She made me lie down on my stomach. On that brown nubbly couch.

NINA: Absolutely I did.

LIZ: Which smelled like dog.

NINA: I made her lie down on the couch and I pulled out every single splinter with a pair of tweezers I had to push the stool over to the medicine cabinet to get. I had kind of forgotten this memory until the first time I saw that Operation game then it all came back to me.

LIZ: I never ever forgot it. I was sobbing.

NINA: She was sort of a cry baby.

LIZ: My feet were like raw hamburger meat by the time you were done with me. *(To Ula)* And I'm sobbing, and she's yelling at me—

NINA: I wasn't yelling but I do remember saying, very sternly: "In this household, we do not say 'ouch.'" Like it was gospel truth. Like it had been said to me a thousand times— even though no one had ever said that to me.

LIZ: And *then* . . .

NINA: And then somehow I knew I had to sterilize the wounds and I couldn't find any hydrogen peroxide so I poured gin over them.

ULA: Oh hey.

LIZ: So painful. And then you probably fixed me breakfast. For breakfast she always made me a bowl of cereal, but she said it was gruel. She gave me usually half as much as

I wanted. And I wanted more. And she always said, if you
want more, you have to say: please sir, may I have some
more gruel.

NINA: In an English accent.

LIZ: In an English accent.

NINA: I had seen *Oliver.* I loved *Oliver.*

LIZ: And so I would. Because I was trained. I wasn't even four,
I didn't know. And one morning Mom was up early and she
made me cereal and I wanted more and I said: "Please sir,
may I have some more gruel."

NINA: In an English accent.

LIZ: In an English accent. And she laughed and laughed.

NINA: It was really funny.

LIZ: Mom made me do it for her friends.

*As they continue to work, we hear this on the overhead
speaker:*

LEN: In the olden days, people ate a lot of corn bread and corn
pone and a lot of the time that could be the main thing
people would eat for days.

Maybe some salt meat or some jerky.

And if you were acquiring nutritional deficiencies by eating the same things all the time . . . normally you didn't
know it. You didn't even know why you were alive anyway
in particular, you'd just been born in some place and so you
made do with that place and the people in it and you didn't
so much think about changing locations.

I think the thing is people were just happy to be eating,
they didn't have that expectation that we have nowadays,
um, expectation . . . the thing where people eat different

things all the time and they really think that there should be a lot of variety all the time and a high quality. Back then you expected food to be delicious only if it was a special occasion and in that case, yes, delicious, but even more important: plentiful.

What really made special occasions exciting were the Bachelors. Bachelors was the term for unattached men who would stumble from the brush and happen across a celebration and get invited in out of politeness. Nowadays when we say "bachelor" we mean a gentleman who for some reason or another hasn't decided to involve himself in matrimony but back then it was the polite term for a man who was really all but an animal. The Bachelors lived on corn pone and salt beef in the brush. Most of them couldn't even make a biscuit. They'd go crazy for biscuits. A Bachelor just in from the brush could put away half of the food you'd made for everybody and if there was a rarity or a delicacy he wouldn't think anything of taking it into a corner and wrapping his arms around it to protect it and hogging it all to himself. And he didn't mean to be rude, that was just a man who had lost every social instinct and was hungry. They were hapless in a way, but a real problem. Because they would eat up every good thing.

CASEY: And are there still Bachelors?

LEN: Now there are ants. Like that little guy there, see. He wants your potato chip.

A considering pause.

CASEY: He can have my potato chip.

LEN: Are you sure?

CASEY: Uh-huh. For me, it's just one potato chip, but for him. It's like. If I found a cake in the woods that was as big as a house. With like, candy windows. I'd go *crazy.*

LEN: Well let's hope he doesn't go *craaazy*. I don't know that I want to see a *craaazy* ant.

CASEY: I would *love* to see a *craaazy* ant!

In the kitchen:

NINA: Liz, what are you making now?

LIZ: Rice salad.

ULA: You made that up.

LIZ: No, it's a legitimate kind of a salad. It's wild rice, cranberries—

ULA: Oh, *wild rice*.

LIZ: Now you understand. It's actually more of a Thanksgiving side dish but I found all the ingredients in the cupboard. Maybe from last Thanksgiving.

ULA: Sounds good.

LIZ: I feel like, actually, this is one of those dishes people take a spoonful of and half of the bowl gets uneaten. But it makes the other dishes seem more appealing by contrast.

NINA: It's not on the list though.

LIZ: I know. I was moved to improvise.

NINA: Yeah but we have all of this . . . cooking, to get through. There isn't really time to improvise.

LIZ: This is going to take me two seconds.

NINA: It's already taken you, what, fifteen minutes.

This has gotten electric pretty fast.

LIZ: How is this a big deal.

NINA: I'm just saying, we have all this stuff to get through we need to really stay focused and to not . . . waver.

LIZ: How long is this going to take me?

NINA: I don't know how long it's going to take you, all I know is that it's going to take you longer than you thought it would and then something else which was supposed to happen, and which we agreed would happen, won't happen.

LIZ: Like, what, the fifth variety of cobbler? This is an obscene amount of food. I mean it, there's something grotesque about all this food.

NINA: Food is great. This is a wake.

LIZ: I know how a wake operates; I've read Irish novels too. A wake is for an entire community.

NINA: We are a community.

LIZ: First of all—we are not. We are a reassembled memory of a community. And second of all we're—we're all we are, this is all we are—a community is extra. When someone dies you make all this food not just so that everyone can stuff their face but so there's enough for strangers, surprises; we're a closed circuit. I like eating a lot as much as the next person but it feels wrong to be pretending that this is a meaningful bounty.

Pause.

ULA: She has a point.

NINA: Well, what. Should we not cook? Should we drive in pizzas? Or should we just make another round of fried chicken and guacamole and call it a day? Everyone likes fried chicken and guacamole. That would be great. That would be much more relaxed.

ULA: I'm not saying we shouldn't cook a lot. Of course we should cook a lot. I want to cook a lot.

NINA: We could make salsa. That's easy. That shouldn't stress anyone out.

ULA: I'm just saying why cook like demons. Let's just make more than enough.

LIZ: I know what I wanted to say:

If Sean had died, back in the day, we would have been devastated.

It would have changed us.

But let's not pretend that Sean was still a real part of our lives.

Let's not pretend we actually miss him.

Let's not pretend that our lives have that kind of grandeur anymore.

Liz leaves.

They continue working for a while in silence.

NINA: How is Gary? I feel like . . . he was applying for a tenure track at, um . . . that college Obama went to, right?
ULA: Oh . . .

We split up.
NINA: Oh shit, Ula. Seriously? I'm so sorry. When was this?
ULA: It was *(Counting it)* three years ago. Pretty much. Three years. Four, really.
NINA: Oh. God.

But didn't we . . . four years ago?
ULA: Yeah. Four.
NINA: But we've talked, since then it hasn't been . . .
ULA: Yeah I lied a little bit. I didn't want to get into it just then.
NINA: Oh.

They continue working for a while in silence.

Len enters, carrying a smallish white cardboard box.

LEN: Peg's here.

NINA: Where?

LEN: Showering, she'll be in in a bit. Where should I put him?

ULA: That's Sean?

LEN: In the flesh. Ish.

A moment where everyone contemplates.

NINA: I was picturing something in brass.

LEN: This is how they come unless you pick out a container. No one picked out a container.

ULA *(Tapping the island)*: Put him right here.

NINA: On a work surface?

ULA: It's where he'd be if he were here. Leaning against, not on.

NINA: Oh god. There's a plastic bag in there, right.

LEN: Yeah yeah. He's air tight.

Everyone continues to contemplate.

NINA: Okay we can't march him to the Blue Hole and scatter him from that. He has to be in something. Something pretty or grand or

Scanning wall height:

A Mexican jug? But which one.

ULA *(The concept, not a particular one)*: That seems sort of festive.

NINA: Day of the Deady. Good/bad?

LEN: He had some Mexican ancestry, right? Maybe it's appropriate.

ULA: No it was all Guatemalan.

LEN: I thought he had a great-grandmother who was Mexican.

ULA: He *speculated* that he had a great-grandmother who was Mexican. To explain his great appreciation of mole.

LIZ *(Has been in the doorway for a little bit)*: I don't think we should do it. I bet the Guatemalans hate the Mexicans.

LEN: Sean didn't hate the Mexicans.

ULA: Why do the Guatemalans hate the Mexicans?

LIZ: I don't know, because everyone hates everyone else. Let's not do a Mexican jug.

NINA: No.

ULA: What about, there's that black stoneware jug in the bunkhouse.

NINA: Or there's that pretty yellow jug. With the kind of [frill] around the edge. Where is that.

LIZ: Let's get both and we can pour him back and forth, back and forth, from one to the other, until we decide.

LEN: My When I Die file will be detailed and specific.

NINA: Okay why doesn't everyone . . . keep their eye out. For a container. Which feels somehow, mysteriously, Right.

Until that time he's going to be here, on the counter, in this white cardboard box.

They all look at it a moment.

LIZ: Maybe we should make a tiny tear, with a knife, just to let him breathe a little.

Beat.

NINA: Okay. Yeah. A tiny tear.

Pass me that knife.

Nina opens the box, stands over it for a moment, reaches in and makes a tiny cut in the plastic, refolds the box top.

Would he have wanted us to bake with him? Do you think?
Just a little bit in . . . bread? Or something?

ULA: Oh, no.

LIZ: No.

NINA: No but do you think he would have liked that, I'm serious.

LEN: I love Sean I'm not eating him.

ULA: I don't think

NINA: I'm talking like a teaspoon, a symbolic teaspoon you'd
never know, you couldn't taste it. It would just be there.

. . .

ULA: I'm trying to think about this in the most accurate and
sophisticated way possible . . .

LEN: If we had all been sitting around this table, drunk, at
twenty-five, and we had said to Sean hey, if you die, do you
want us to mix some of your ashes into a loaf of bread and
eat them—would you want that—he would have said hell
yeah, no better way to go. And then he would have spent
the most drunken part of the evening shouting Eat me! Eat
me! and making passes at Suzie until Rory marched him
to bed.

But, if we had been able to speak to him, in his dying
moments in New York, as he lay on the pavement, and say
hey, Sean, remember all of us? We get you when you're
dead, shall we eat you?

I'm not so sure.

There is a pause.

LIZ: I'm going to go look for something for Sean.

She leaves.

LEN: Liz is doing well.
NINA: Liz is a fucking mess.

    She's on six medications.
LEN: Oh.
NINA: Oh Jesus Christ, Len—where's Casey?
LEN: Adrian's got her.
NINA: Adrian?
LEN: They're in the yard. He said he'd spell me.
NINA: I should go rescue Adrian. He really doesn't like children.

She exits.

LEN: Not that I wasn't enjoying the Quality Audience. I've got
    a lot of wisdom, as it turns out.
ULA: Yeah kids are good that way.

Lights out on the island. We hear this on the speakers:

NINA: Oh Casey, there you are. Adrian.
CASEY: I'm in the *yard*, Mom.
NINA: I know.
CASEY: I'm not near the river *or* the cactus patch. Did you see
    our cactus patch?
ADRIAN: I did. It's very impressive. Lots of spikes.
CASEY: Lots and LOTS of spikes.
NINA: Whatshuguys doin'?
CASEY: We're looking at this ant. We made an executive deci-
    sion about the potato chip.
NINA: What was that?
CASEY: Well the ants were *very* interested in the potato chip, but
    they were spending a lot of time arguing about it with their
    tentacles *(Corrects herself)* antennae.

ADRIAN: And we didn't want there to be an ant war.

CASEY: We didn't want there to be an ant war. So we decided, that we would break the potato chip into a hundred little pieces.

And it's sort of like we're playing God. But giving them the potato chip in the first place is like playing God, because they've never seen a potato chip before. Or it's sort of like playing aliens from outer space. And so we broke it into a hundred little pieces.

ADRIAN: Exactly a hundred.

CASEY: Or, approximately a hundred. And so each ant can have its own potato chip piece. And *now*, we're watching them take them back to the nest—to the *hill*. And we're looking at the first ant and we're seeing if he gets there first because it was his potato chip to begin with, I gave it to him, and he should get the credit for it. *She*, ants are shes, she should get the credit for it. But right now there's another ant ahead.

NINA: Which ant is the first one?

CASEY: That one.

NINA: And that ant is going faster.

ADRIAN: Quite a bit faster, at this point.

A bit of watching.

NINA: Are you sure this is the right ant? Maybe the ant which is ahead, is really the ant you gave the potato chip to in the first place.

CASEY: I'm sure Mom.

Bit of a watchful silence.

NINA: Ouch.

Little bugger.

CASEY: Mom, what did you do?!

NINA: An ant was biting me.

CASEY: Did you kill him??

NINA: Honey, when he bit me I brushed him off me.

CASEY: Is he okay???

NINA: You know, I don't know, they're kind of fragile.

CASEY *(Furious)*: Mom! Mommy! I *can't believe* that you killed that ant!

NINA: Honey, this wasn't one of your ants this was one of those little tiny bitey ones.

CASEY: Mom it doesn't matter what kind of ant he is; now that ant is dead! And it will never never never never be alive again.

And think, think about what you did because his mommy is going to be crying now.

Increasing rising hysteria.

I can't believe you did that!!

Runs away.

NINA: Casey!

ADRIAN *(Urgent)*: I would leave her be.

NINA: Casey! Adrian, Jesus, let go my arm.

ADRIAN: Nina. Just let her go.

NINA: I need to see what direction she's going in . . . to her cabin . . . fine . . .

For your information. She wants to jump into the Blue Hole. From the side. *He's* terrified. She wants to jump right now.

ADRIAN: Is that so terrible?

NINA: She's tiny. And I've been telling her no. And yesterday she just ran right up to the side—and jumped right off. And

I jumped in after her and hauled her out up the side—which is actually really hard to do, but there's all that adrenaline. I said we're marching right back.

Her brother was whining, because he never even got to go in. And I turned to him and said: tough luck buddy which is something I have never said before. And I said no Blue Hole for you for the whole time this visit!

And I felt like God when I said it, or a wrathful Moses coming down from the mountain, I felt so *right*, and that was such a pleasure, honestly, I was *right*, but, she was SO mad. So angry.

Now, I feel like, she's going to make me pay, for that pleasure. And I'm terrified she's going to go on her own. Go up there on her own just to go. And I can't stop her. How can I stop her? And if she *realizes*, when she realizes I'm trying to stop her then, really . . . nothing will stop her.

A little beat.

Adrian was there a way to stop you. When you were set on something.
ADRIAN: Me?
NINA: There wasn't a way to persuade you. Otherwise.
ADRIAN: There was buying me another drink. Apparently.
NINA: Apart from . . . guile. Apart from pretending. Lying. Manipulating.
ADRIAN: You could have just given in to me. You could have just said yes, yes.
NINA: That would have meant craziness. And often: danger. Real danger. Did you really want that? In your heart of hearts? I always thought no. But later on I thought, probably, actually . . .

ADRIAN *(Suddenly)*: What would your mom have done?

NINA: What would Mom?

ADRIAN: Casey wants to jump into the Blue Hole. What would your mom have done?

NINA: The wrong thing.

ADRIAN: There's a bit of your mom in her, right?

NINA: Oh my god. She's all Mom. She's actually there's this saving grace streak of Adam but yes. Genetics sucks. I gave birth to my mother.

ADRIAN *(Suddenly)*: What would your mom have done.

NINA: You're serious.

ADRIAN: It's only a question, Nina. Just ask it.

NINA: It's a dumb question. I have spent my entire life trying to *not* be my mother.

ADRIAN: I know.

NINA: My entire life.

ADRIAN: The dead are dead, Nina, right? Your mom's gone. She doesn't own you.

She can't eat you.

Bit of a pause.

NINA: What would Mom have done . . .

what would Mom have done . . .

Oh . . . I don't know . . .

God I wish she were here, to be the bad glamorous grandmother.

Casey is a cutie though, isn't she, even if she's a terror.

ADRIAN: She is indeed. *(Laughs)* And she is going to be a Troubling Beauty.

NINA: Yeah. Yeah. Not looking forward to it. What did you guys talk about.

ADRIAN: Oh, lots of things. She asked me about God.

NINA: Casey asked you about God. Really?

ADRIAN: Uh-huh.

NINA: Huh. What did you tell her?

He laughs.

What did you tell her Adrian?

Casey sings.

As the song continues, she is joined by a chorus, and by musics until it is no longer her song at all.

CASEY:
Poor dead little guys.

Poor dead little guys. Now the poor ant is dead.

Poor ant is dead . . .

Poor ant is dead

The sun shall crown his head

In the earth he makes his bed

This sad, little ant, is dead

This sweet little ant has gone

From the earth which he walked upon

Rest his weary head

This sad / tender ant / is dead

The darling ant did die

And the glimmer of her eye

Has dulled

The sweet sproing of all her limbs

Has ceased

When from this savage world / she was / released

And a fanatic walks among us

A man from desert lands

He parts his lips to roar

His song is winds and sands.

The stage is dark and blank.

Very low and whispery and intimate still on the speaker:

ADRIAN: I want you . . . to wake up now
NINA: Hmmmph.
ADRIAN: I want you to wake up
NINA: Mmmmmgh?
ADRIAN: I want to show you something.
NINA: Ah. What are you doing here.
ADRIAN: Come on. Get up.

NINA: Get up? No. Get out.

ADRIAN: I have something to show you.

NINA: What are you doing here?

ADRIAN: There's something you need to see. Outside.

NINA: I'm naked.

ADRIAN: Well get dressed then. And meet me out there.

He is standing outside.

She joins him.

We see them at first only in silhouette.

There are stars.

NINA: Are we looking at the stars? Because they're nice, but I've
    seen them.

ADRIAN: We're looking at just a few stars in particular.

NINA: Wait are we awake, or asleep?

ADRIAN: What do you think?

NINA: I don't know. There's that warm wind. It kind of feels like
    a dream.

ADRIAN: You're just sleepy, you're bleary.

NINA: I am.

ADRIAN: Find the Big Dipper

NINA: Yeah, okay, got it, that was easy.

ADRIAN: Now from the very tip of the handle, and all the way
    down, to the very edge of the horizon.

NINA: Uh-huh.

ADRIAN: That one there, that one there, that one there, and that
    one there.

NINA: . . .

Where? What am I looking at?

ADRIAN: I'm pointing right at it but it doesn't matter, you can't see it. Not because it's too faint—although it's very very faint—but because your eyes can't make sense of it it has no natural shape.

It's Antlia Pneumatica—the air pump.

NINA: The what?

ADRIAN: Air pump.

NINA: Where?

ADRIAN: You're looking right at it.

It was named by a French astronomer I don't remember his name. In the 1700s. He pulled together leftover stars and made new constellations.

NINA: The air pump.

ADRIAN: There's a microscope, an engraving tool, a ship's compass a . . . "chemical furnace." They're extremely faint. They. None of them look anything like the name. He dibsed them. He dibsed them just to dibs them. To leave his mark.

NINA: I don't see it.

ADRIAN: You can't see it. It took me hours to see it. Now I can't not see it, when it's in season, I can't look away.

Pause.

NINA: Why are you showing me this? Thing which I can't see.

ADRIAN: Because when we know that four stars have been slung together and called an air pump, we realize that really, the whole sky is up for grabs.

We make it all up, everything we believe in. And what we make, we can unmake. And remake. I find it . . . liberating.

Bit of a beat.

NINA: Okay, yes. Except. The stars are real. The stars are actually happening. They're facts.

ADRIAN: Are they? By the time we see them? They're facts in the past. For all we know all they are now is just, light. Visual noise. Incident. Nothing.

NINA: Hmph.

ADRIAN: That constellation there. Do you know it?

NINA: Which one.

ADRIAN: That bright star, that's an eye, and that bright one there, that's also an eye. I'm going to get a little Picasso with this but there there there—let's call that a kind of triangulated mouth. Open. And the Milky Way is hair. See it?

NINA: Okay. Right. That's a big one.

ADRIAN: Do you recognize it?

NINA: Of course not.

ADRIAN: Nina.

NINA: What?

ADRIAN: From now on: Nina.

Pause.

NINA: Oh.

You've just commandeered pretty much the entire sky. For that constellation there.

ADRIAN: Nina. There, there, there there there and—the Milky Way. Whenever you look up into the sky now, you're going to see it, you're going to see yourself, you can't help it.

Pause.

NINA: Only when I'm out here. In L.A. I'll be just, two eyes.

ADRIAN: That's enough.

NINA: It's . . . creepy I think.

I feel like we look at the sky to get away from ourselves.

ADRIAN: You won't forget this. Even though it isn't a fact.

You'll always see the sky differently.

NINA: And you enjoy that, don't you.

ADRIAN: I do. Yes. I do.

NINA: Nina. The Enormous. Looking down on myself.

I'm so far away.

ADRIAN: You're right here.

NINA: You're holding my hand.

ADRIAN: Oh—

He looks down.

Yes. I am.

I lied to you. About time. It *is* an illusion.

You're a dim dwindled memory, and you're also right here.
You're my distant past, *and* you're my girl.

A moment.

NINA: It's cold. I should get back in.

ADRIAN: It isn't cold at all.

NINA: I should get back in.

ADRIAN: Do you need to? If you're dreaming?

NINA: Am I dreaming?

ADRIAN: Doesn't it feel like a dream? That wind.

Little pause.

NINA: You know, there's a dream I used to have about you. For
    years afterwards. We'd be some place, wherever, and it
    was all very ordinary we were together. And then at some

point—maybe things would get a little strange anyway there would be a moment, in the dream, where we would realize that it was a dream, and we'd admit that we were dreaming about each other.

And I'd say where are you, really, and you'd say I'm in your bed, I'm in your bed right next to you. And I'd say really? And you'd say yes, wake up. And I'd wake up and you weren't.

Little pause.

When that happened, I used to wonder if you were dreaming it too.

Little pause.

ADRIAN: I don't ever remember my dreams.

Little pause.

NINA: No. I remember that.

You're going to fade away again, aren't you. Into your own. Particular. Mists.
ADRIAN: Let's go back to your bed
NINA: Oh. No.
ADRIAN: I want your face to be the first thing I see in the first light.

From Nina: an involuntary "oh."

Those mornings. I had no idea they were precious. I used to look at you sometimes, you were still asleep, sometimes you had some foam at your lips—you were sort of a drooler—and your face was puffy and I knew your breath was stale—it was kind of disgusting.

NINA: Wow. Wow.

ADRIAN: Not the thoughts of a man in love, I know. At least, it seemed that way to me at the time.

NINA: Were you in love with me at all?

ADRIAN: I was as in love with you as it was possible for me to be please believe me.

NINA: I was so in love with you.

ADRIAN: I knew that.

NINA: Were you in love with me at all?

ADRIAN: I knew my destiny. It was a woman who could speak perfect semi-gutter Spanish, when she wanted to, barely an accent, with long curly dark hair which she put up and then pulled down and then put up again, a woman who could drink like a maniac but usually didn't, who didn't think much of me, in a lot of ways, but could totally drink me in, accept me completely, at moments I couldn't antici-pate. Who would drive me over the border to back-street taquerias and order us fantastic meals without the menu, a woman the men would leer at in a way that was almost dangerous, and when we got back we would make love in a room filled with luminaria she'd picked up at botanicas and bodegas and the Walmart, luminaria which were ironic and sincere and ironic and vivid, glowing. A woman who loved and hated God.

Or an indie rocker from Austin who fronted her own band and had some great secret tattoos.

I had different moods.

NINA: And did you meet her?

ADRIAN: I met both of them, well, with variants. But I didn't feel the way I thought I would. Like when you go to a museum

and there's a painting and it's famous and you stand in front
of it and it doesn't quite do it for you.

They weren't what I hoped or I wasn't what I hoped but
I didn't really mind—all that time, what I most wanted
was to wake up in so many different beds and see the sky
through windows I didn't recognize with pieces of skyline
I'd never seen.

I wanted to know as much as anyone could possibly know.
I wanted every experience.

Women were crucial, but they were the least important crucial thing. They weren't the motor they weren't the vehi-
cle they were the landscape I was going to be traveling
through.

NINA: And it didn't matter to you if you left some tire tracks. On
that . . . landscape.

ADRIAN: I didn't want clean breaks, I wanted to be remembered,
and sometimes the best way to be remembered is to make
a little mayhem; leave a little scar. The place where I was.

An epitaph.

To my credit: I believed that the women I was with were
women who loved graves, scars.

Women who loved sorrow.

Women who would happily endure that kind of eerie wretch-
edness rather than, whatever, the mundane.

NINA: And you thought that I was one of those women. Who
loved scars. Sorrow. Graves.

ADRIAN: Didn't you love me? And wasn't I a wicked man?

His hand on her face.

They move toward each other.

The stars behind them have been brightening in intensity during this, until the stage is almost a wash of light.

TOTAL BLACKOUT.

In the blackout:

The brother and sister discuss:

CASEY *(Menacing Wally)*: What if the moon doesn't come back?
WALLY *(Stoutly)*: The moon always comes back.
CASEY: What if the moon has been eaten this month, by a bad sneaky star.
WALLY: Then we'll build a new one. We're Texas.

The kitchen, the island, day.

ULA: Morning, Sunshine.
NINA: How did it get to be so late?
ULA: You just slumbered and slumbered and slumbered.
NINA: But where's Casey and Wally?
LEN: Up bright and early.
NINA *(Still bleary)*: They're my little alarm systems. Clocks. Where are they?
LEN: In the back. Playing.

Nina looks over to the counter, looks around.

NINA: Hey, where *is* Sean?
LEN: Sean is . . . not there. Ula did you move Sean?

ULA: Um . . . no. He wasn't there an hour ago though, when I was spreading everything out.

LEN: Liz must have him. Maybe she found a container and is trying him out for size.

NINA: Did the kids get breakfast?

LEN: Yes. *Wally* wanted a bowl of cereal. I gave him a bowl of cereal, and bacon. Which he happily accepted. Casey said that she would not have the bacon, but she would have the cereal. But when I gave her the cereal she brought it back and said could she have a bowl without milk in it. I said you have to drink your milk, Casey, you're a growing girl—I did that part right, right?

NINA: Yeah that's all good.

She has poured, and is lightly doctoring, a coffee.

LEN: And she said I won't have milk. And I figured, well, I'm not Enforcement here.

NINA: Uh uh.

LEN: I did touch—very lightly—upon the not wasting good food lecture I remember from my childhood, leaving out Ethiopia. But it was lighthearted. Just wanted to make sure that ground was covered in case you're doing that.

NINA: Right.

LEN: And I gave her a new bowl of cereal. And she sat in front of it on the table and finally she brought it back to me and said I should pour it back into the box because she wasn't going to eat it.

And I said can I make you toast. And she said no. And I said you're sure you don't want bacon. And she said no bacon. And I said what about a package of instant oatmeal with *strawberries* in it. Little freeze-dried strawberries. And fake powdered cream. Yum.

And she said no.

And I said, Casey, you have to eat.

And she said I do not wish the death of any creature.

And I said but honey, oatmeal is not a creature.

And she said any being that wished to live, is a creature.

And I said oh honey, that oatmeal does not care if it lives or dies, believe me.

And she said, how do you know that?

You don't know that.

We just pretend to know what other things want. So we don't have to think about it. Because if we think about it, maybe what they want

. . . and here it was sort of amazing I saw her trembling on the very verge of the word "inconvenient" but she couldn't quite get there . . .

maybe what they want, isn't what we want.

Nothing should have to die, if it doesn't want to.

Nothing should have to die ever!!

And I said, but honey, if you don't eat *something*, you'll be *hungry*, and then *you'll* die—this was totally lighthearted and merry by the way, totally not scary or intimidating— I said: that would be sort of ironic, right?

ULA: Woah. What did she say?

LEN: She got very very quiet.

And then she said—wait for this: it was very beautiful. She said:

"God loves the Hungry."

NINA AND ULA *(More or less simultaneously, more of a sound than a word)*: Wow.

LEN: And then she went kind of sailing out.

And then Wally said may I be excused and I said certainly. As though I were the ruler of Excused. Although he had eaten *everything* so why not. I kind of like parenting. It's sort of a ride.

NINA: Huh. *That's* a new phase.

ULA: It's pretty Deep. "God loves the Hungry."

LEN: Right??

ULA: Does this child have religious training?

NINA: No you guys it's just The Deep Phase. A little ahead of schedule.

ULA: The Deep Phase. Right.

LEN: I was a very deep child. In my—as a child—opinion.

ULA: Please. No one understood me. No one. I was very mysterious.

NINA: I remember one time I went to my dad—I was always going to my dad and trying to impress him with my deep thoughts—and I told him that I had just been listening to the wind in the pecans, not the big ones by the river but that orchard, and that I had realized that right now, for the wind, it's like, we're giving it a little harmonica to play on, with some of the prongs gone, but when those pecans are grown, it's like it's going to have a tremendous guitar, and it can say everything it wants to say.

And he said aw honey, it's not trying to impress us, or express itself, it's just trying to get from here to there without stumbling over all those leaves.

That kid's a voracious trencherman. She loves bacon. She'll be back.

Small beat.

LEN: You know, this is the most I've ever heard you talk about your dad. The most. By far. This visit.
NINA: Oh, um. Right. I didn't did I. Habit.

People used to really want to know and that was creepy I mean normal but still gross and . . . I just didn't want it to be a point of interest. I wanted to be the point of interest.

Kind of a pause.

ULA: I swiped one of your dad's coffee cups. Do you remember, the one I said I broke? When you said Oh those are my dad's don't use those and I said sorry. I took it.
NINA: Which one?
ULA: The sort of gray clay one with the dark blue blots on it.
NINA: You don't still have it, do you?
ULA: I do. I do somewhere. Probably in storage. *(Mini pause)* Do you want it back?
NINA: *No.* I just remember it. I'm glad it's out there somewhere in the world.
ULA: It wasn't his favorite one was it? I was too guilty to ask.
NINA: I don't think he even noticed it was gone.
ULA: You know this is a major confession. Not in the big emotional sense, I mean, I'm not going to cry or anything and I hope you aren't either but it does come from the Major

Confession box where it has been living for all of these years.

NINA: I think . . . if I had known about that at the time . . . I would have felt Betrayed. Now, I don't care one bit. I feel like: of course you did, I would have done the same.

LEN: I always hoped we'd come and he'd accidentally be here. A little bit of glamour is fun, in friends. When you're young. Now I find that larger-than-life people are a chore.

NINA: See? But you lied to me at the time and that's all that's important. I never knew.

ULA: Thank god. So what we were discussing. Before you wandered in—and you're welcome to join in at any point, by the way.

NINA: I'm there. I'm there at any moment. I'll do peaches. I'm there post bowl of cereal. Five minutes.

She wanders off, gets cereal, milk.

ULA: Is the plan for this funeral. I feel like we don't have enough of a plan for this funeral. We have sunset, and afterwards a feast. Shouldn't there be music, for instance? Should we take the boom box up?

LEN: He wasn't a fan of your dad's, if that's consoling.

NINA: Damn, what would Sean want us to play, in a tinny boom box.

Liz has come in, heads for coffee. Ula fills her in.

Music for the funeral, right?

LIZ: Definitely.

NINA: What's a song Sean really liked . . .

ULA: That's so strange to me, that I can't remember anything he really really loved.

LEN: I have a very strong memory of him jiggling in time to something. With enthusiasm. But I don't remember what.

NA: We can't *make* music can we?

ᴇɴ: I can still kind of play the piano.

ᴌA: Can Scott still play guitar do you think?

z: There are some old acoustics around, and strings and such, but he'd have to know how to tune them.

ɴA: Adrian. Adrian can play.

ᴌA: Oh right.

Yes. Of course.

Micro-beat.

NINA: And we should *sing* something, shouldn't we? We should sing.

LEN: We probably *should* sing. What on earth should we sing?

LIZ: A song for the dead . . .

There is a moment of blank. Then:

ULA: Liz *you* have Sean, right?

LIZ: Me?

ULA: We thought you had him with you. On a container search.

LIZ: *Oh.* No. I haven't found anything yet. *(Looking around)* He didn't go walkabout?

LEN: He's not where he was . . .

NINA: You don't think Casey . . . ?

She goes to the window.

Len has been thinking.

LEN: He wasn't here this morning. When the kids came in. Because I was parking the milk right . . . there. And I believe that I would have instinctively shifted, the milk for the children, *away* from the dead body.

ULA: Well he must be here *somewhere.*
LIZ: Maybe Adrian has him.

Nina is looking out the window.

NINA: Adrian's car's not out there.
ULA: Yeah but it never came back from the spin out, did it? Did
    he end up getting it towed?
NINA: I guess so . . . no that's right I didn't see it yesterday.
LEN: I didn't see it on the road when I drove to town. So.
NINA: Whatever they are doing, they are very intent. Fossil
    hunting?
LIZ: Casey wants to be flower girl. She's picking petals.
NINA: Not a lot of petals out there.
LIZ: Yeah I mentioned that. She said she'd find a whole basket
    of them.
NINA: Oh hell.
ULA: I smell a meltdown . . .
LEN: Quick, do a parenting thing.
NINA: Jesus, Len.
LEN: If you're not up to the task I'm happy to give it a whirl.

A beat.

NINA: What . . . would Mother . . . do . . .
LIZ: Mom? Really?
NINA: I know . . . I know
LIZ: Our mom?
NINA: Uh-huh

Opens them.

    Oh holy god I don't know. Something crazy
LIZ: Yes.

Nina shuts her eyes.

It takes a moment.

NINA: She . . . would . . . put together . . . a very glamorous crazy
outfit . . . with a veil and uh . . .

*Waves her hands about in the air, she sees it, she's trying
to express it.*

. . . and with traily things . . . and when Casey came back
to the house, weeping, with this little tiny handful of petals, she would clap her into the outfit *and* she would have
the fanciest dish ready for the petals except she would have
fruit in it, cut-up pretty fruit in it, watermelon, mango, and
she would have Casey *sprinkle* the flower petals on it, and
spices, like, red and yellow spices—I know we have some
turmeric, and I think some paprika

Eyes open.

Oh my god, and she'd pour tequila all over it, from a little
tiny pitcher—she'd have Casey do it, at the grave site and
then she'd let Casey light it on fire—while she's wearing
all these floaty flammable things—and intone: Sean, these
sweet offerings are for you, take them into the afterlife.
With the love we bear you.

(To Liz) Right??

A beat.

LIZ: Sounds Mom to me.
NINA: She's a mad genius.
LEN: She is indeed.

Nina looks around.

NINA: Okay, it would help that she would have her wardrobe to work from.

ULA: Ask Suzie.

NINA: I'm going to ask Suzie. And there *are* some . . . curtains?

ULA: Gold . . . rickrack!

NINA: None of that here. Mom would have a gold belt, like a slim snaky-looking gold belt. But maybe, in the shed, I think there's some brass chain . . .

ULA: Lipstick!

NINA: Yes!

ULA: Do you have lipstick?

NINA: No. But Peg will!

ULA: Red, we need red.

NINA: I'm *sure* Peg has red lipstick on her.

ULA: Excellent!

Nina runs off to assemble outfit.

(Calling after her) And smoky blue eyeliner! Suzie has some!

They continue working.

Sound of a car pulling up on the gravel outside.

LEN: Who's that?

ULA: You know what I bet. I bet that's Adrian. I bet he's been out all night.

LEN: Out all night where.

ULA: Out all night . . . somewhere.

LIZ: That's true, actually. He could always find a place to be out very late at night. Wherever it was.

*The woman who enters has a fairly noticeable South Caro-
lina accent.*

BAMA: Look at you. Look at all of you.

ULA: Bama!

General hugs and greetings.

You're so early aren't you? Didn't your plane just land?

BAMA: Do you know what I did? I said: fuck it. I just hate early
morning flights, hate 'em hate 'em, I flew in to San Antonio last night, booked one of those hotels right next to the
airport.

Had a whole long hot bath all to myself, not one single
interruption from a small person, it was heaven. I told Erik
I just had to leave earlier because the ceremony was resched-
uled for very early in the morning with the dawn breaking
and I said—I lied. I just lied. I made up crazy details.

LIZ: Hungry?

BAMA: *No.* Because then what I did, this morning, because I had
spied, down the road from my hotel, a *Denny's. (There is
a general: "Ohhhhhhh.")* And I think, because I've been
thinking, you know, about Sean, and about all of you, it
was like I was twenty-five again or my central nervous sys-
tem was deceived so I just *went* to Denny's and I got that
thing, with all of those *parts.*

ULA: Oh the

BAMA: With *everything.*

LEN: Right. Right. The *everything.*

BAMA: With the hot cakes and the eggs *(Pronouncing "aigs")* and
the syrup and the hash browns and the bacon and the grits
and butter it was just it was just ridiculous and the orange
juice and I think I ate most of it and little jelly packets.

ULA: Oh. Yeah.

BAMA: I just ate the whole thing. But I will take coffee, if there is coffee going.

LIZ: There is coffee going.

BAMA: That is music to my ears. Oh my gosh this is like. This is like and you don't any of you look any different to me except for the hairstyles which is just sad because do you remember *(To Ula)* do you remember when we were wait-staffing for that event at the university for that reunion event and it was for, it was for their twentieth or their twenty-fifth do you remember that?

ULA: I don't . . .

BAMA: It was a morning breakfast event (Oh thank you. So much) and I can't . . . because they were so irredeemably old they were our age they were so irredeemably old so I didn't even care: twentieth, twenty-fifth, no distinction it was too late for them are you sure you don't remember? You were in charge of a coffee carafe, I was bussing.

ULA: It all blurs together for me, all that wait-staffing.

BAMA: You were probably hungover

ULA: I was probably very hungover

BAMA: I don't know why they ever gave you a carafe in the morning it was a miracle you never scalded anyone this is great by the way Liz, thank you.

LIZ: Oh I just poured it this is Len's coffee.

BAMA: Len this is great coffee.

LEN: Thank you Bama.

BAMA: Okay well the point is, that event, all these people, these old old people, they kept rushing up to each other and saying you haven't changed! You haven't changed! You look just the same! You looked at me and you said, very dry, you said *(Starts to laugh ahead of it)* "macular degeneration." *(Finishes laughing)*

ULA: Oh god.

BAMA: And now you look just the same to me, you all do, it's just pathetic, who else is here, did Rory end up coming?

ULA: Rory couldn't make it. Carlos couldn't make it. Karinne couldn't make it. Maddie couldn't make it. I couldn't locate Sally. It's us, Peg, Suzie, Scott is coming in this afternoon. And *Adrian* is here.

A bit of a weird beat.

BAMA: Adrian?

LEN: I know. He called up out of the blue.

Another bit of a weird beat.

BAMA: Nina's Adrian?

LIZ: Ex. The ex Adrian.

BAMA: Of course. Yes. Is here? Adrian is here?

ULA: He got here, day before yesterday.

BAMA: Here. Right now.

ULA: Yup.

LEN: Or: in the vicinity.

ULA: He had a weird weird story.

LEN: Adrian always had a weird story. Although the weirdest part about them was that they always turned out to be true.

BAMA: Okay I . . . would like to sit down.

LIZ: Bama are you okay?

LEN: Do you feel okay?

BAMA *(On sitting down)*: You know, this doesn't actually help.

LIZ: Do you want a water? Or?

BAMA: Oh. *No.* No I'm fine, I just. I just need to. Recombobulate.

I'm fine I really am I just, I thought: Adrian.

LEN: I know. It's been surprisingly easy.

ULA: It's been a little too easy.

LEN *(Not more than partly ironic; more of a statement of intent)*:
I think everything is just fine.

BAMA: I'm sure. Oh I'm sure. I mean. Right. *(Looks around at
everyone)* I have to tell you something.

A bit of a hanging pause.

And now I just really wish that I'd just kept my cool and
been: huh. I cannot keep a reaction inside of my body it
really is a problem, actually, I used to think it was just a
foible now I think . . . that it has actually worked to my
detriment in more of a major way throughout my life.
I. Three years ago I was on a site visit to a treatment center
a narcotics treatment center in Arizona, Western Arizona, it
was a program audit—anyway. I'm actually not involved
with that whole side of it anymore but I was on a site visit
and as part of the sets of paperwork and whatnot I was
going through there was this list of patients who had been
discharged, over the course of the last year, and outcomes.
And. Adrian was on that list.

ULA: Oh. Wow.

This was three years ago?

BAMA: Three years ago. Adrian was on the list. And he was
listed as deceased. As of two weeks previous.

ULA: Oh my god.

LEN: So this whole time—

ULA: You've been thinking . . .

BAMA: It's not such a common name so I pulled strings. And
I went to the morgue—no one had claimed the body—and
they let me look at him.

And I could have sworn it was him. I mean people's faces,
death.

There was this huge tattoo on his chest, all over his chest and his stomach big black lettering: "set me on fire," "set me on fire" that was all I could really see I guess, so.

And I thought: Oh, I should tell Nina, right, but I put it off a bit and then Mom was diagnosed and the next four months was all about the hospital, and hospice and at the end of it all I had just I had actually just completely forgotten. It was right out of my head until I heard about Sean and then. And I thought surely, by this time surely Nina knows. I mean I guess I didn't want to be the person to say you know, by the way, three *years* ago, so but then I thought you know what, I'll get there, I'll sort of find out and if she doesn't know then I'll tell her in person. And now, I don't have to. So hurrah.

Pause.

I am so glad, I didn't tell Nina.

LEN: "Set me on fire"?

BAMA: Oh it was. I don't know it was: if I die, set me afire, something like that, let me go up in flames, bring on the whirlwind, something like that. Something very Adrian. I even remember I thought something like: "oh you, you *would* go ahead and do, something like that . . ."

Do you know what? I mean: my mouth, my big big mouth. I think, and this is maturity, because it's kind of a *great* story and if I were ten or even five years younger I would *absolutely* have told it, to *everyone*, and most especially to Nina and Adrian but do you know what I think I think I am not going to mention this to anyone, especially to Nina, and to Adrian.

I feel like this is one of those things you actually don't want to blurt out.

Micro-pause.

LIZ: No.

Len speaks to the audience:

LEN: There's one story of a Bachelor who came out of the brush and there was a funeral. And so of course he was invited inside, Mr. Decker was his name, and Alice, the lady of the house, she tactfully invited him into the kitchen so he could take his meal there and he wouldn't have to feel uncomfortable among the other guests with his big muddy boots and his patched damp coat. She sat him right down on one end of the kitchen table where they were setting out all the dishes that were to be brought into the other room. "You help yourself Mr. Decker," she told him, and she sat a big plate of biscuits by him, and she made him a plate with sliced ham and with pickles.

Mr. Decker sat right down and commenced to work his way steadily through a big plate of biscuits. Maizie, the eldest child of the household, a girl of seven, had also been sat down for her dinner, and after a little while she said, "Would you mind passing me the plate of biscuits Mr. Decker?" "In a bit child," he said, "in a bit. I'm still going at them. Hand me the plate of ham will you? For ham and biscuits I think go extremely well together. And maybe make me up a napkin of those good fried chicken legs, I wouldn't want to tax your fine china here."

And shortly afterwards Alice returned to the kitchen to discover that he had fastened particularly on the pound cake which was a great delicacy in that time. He was cutting big thick slices and dipping them into gravy—right into the gravy bowl, actually—and kind of shoveling them into his mouth with alternately slices of ham, and legs of fried chicken.

And she said, "Oh, Mr. Decker, wouldn't you like some more of these *biscuits*?"—she was a little bit desperate about the pound cake—and he said, "No ma'am, you save the rest of that for your guests, this here yaller bread will do me just fine."

At that moment she was called into the front room—and I should have mentioned earlier that it was raining very steadily, and had been all afternoon—by the arrival of a late guest, drenchingly wet, and with a very serious expression on his face. And the other guests asked what was wrong and he said, "'Pon my word, there's been a very serious accident on the Upper Willow Creek crossing, the currents is so bad there now that a wagon would have a hard time fording it, and an individual trying to cross it this afternoon fell into the deluge when his horse stumbled, and was swept away; we expect his body to fetch up sometime tomorrow."

When did this accident occur? Asked one guest. And, isn't there any thought of his survival? Asked another guest hopefully.

The accident occurred some hours ago, the newcomer averred and I am afraid, ma'am, he continued, that there is no hope at all for the poor fellow, for the individual in question is known to be a man entirely unable to swim.

Why what is the name of this poor soul?! Asked all gathered, in some consternation and wonderment.

Why the ol' Bachelor known by the name of Decker, who lives out in the bush yonder.

With that there was a terrible shriek from Alice and all turned towards her. She was not looking at the bearer of sad tidings, however, but into the kitchen, and when she turned to the company her face was as white as a sheet, whether from terror or from rage it was difficult to say.

"That ghost ate up all of my fried chicken and pound cake!" she cried.

A big huge rustling of lots of winds in big fully crowned trees.

They all sing:

ALL:

> There was that night the stars enlarged
> There was that night the stars exploded
> The night we danced as fire-y bits about us fell and
>   smoldered
> Your face was ecstasy
> That night you looked at me
> And said you know I think maybe I'm loaded
>
> That night you tore off your jean jacket
> And you roared unto the moon
> You said I feel it rising in me
> You said my day is coming soon
>
> The moon ignited on the river
> Underneath a ravaged sky
> We awakened in the morning
> And our splendor passed us by

And much more than we can say
And so much we can't remember
We thought the rain would never come
And that the drought would last forever
We thought that thirst would overcome us
And that we would long forever

And you dried up and blew away
When you fell asleep forever
Now the rain has finally come
And you are carried to the river

And the pecans drink you in
And when the winds rush through them
You'll find the song you never had
Of struggle and of ruin
The extraordinary song
Of surging towards the light, and ruin.

The song ends, all take their bows, and leave the stage.

END

ANNE WASHBURN's plays include *10 Out of 12, Antlia Pneumatica, Apparition, The Communist Dracula Pageant, A Devil at Noon, I Have Loved Strangers, Mr. Burns, Shipwreck, The Internationalist, The Ladies, The Small*, an adaptation of *The Twilight Zone*, and transadaptations of Euripides' *Orestes* and *Iphigenia in Aulis*. Her work has been produced nationally and internationally and has premiered with 13P, Actors Theatre of Louisville, The Almeida Theatre, American Repertory Theater, Cherry Lane Theatre, Classic Stage Company, Clubbed Thumb, The Civilians, Dixon Place, Ensemble Studio Theatre, Folger Theatre, Playwrights Horizons, Soho Rep., Two River Theater, Vineyard Theatre, and Woolly Mammoth Theatre Company. Honors include a Guggenheim Fellowship, a Whiting Award, an Alpert Award, a PEN/Laura Pels Award for an American Playwright in Mid-Career, a NYFA Fellowship, a Time Warner Fellowship, and residencies at The MacDowell Colony and Yaddo. She is an associated artist with The Civilians, Clubbed Thumb, New Georges, and an alumna of New Dramatists.